Time Management

The Role Of Productivity And Self-discipline In
Overcoming Procrastination, Maximizing Time Efficiency,
And Achieving Personal Freedom

*(Develop Proficiency In Time Management, Overcome And
Vanquish Procrastination)*

Mirosław Daniel

TABLE OF CONTENT

Learning To Delegate 1

What Constitutes Significance And Priority? 11

Take A Lunch Break 18

Efficient Strategies For Time Management 36

Exploring Strategies To Implement Your Objectives
.... 46

Establishing Deadlines For Your Assignments 55

The Significance Of A Task List For Achieving Short-Term And Long-Term Objectives 67

Achieving Proficiency In A Time Management System 73

Mitigating Distractions And Time-Consuming Activities 85

Learning Time Management 106

The Detriments Of Time Management 114

Making Lists 127

The Significance Of Prioritization In Time Management 134

Learning To Delegate

There exist individuals who exhibit a strong inclination towards possessiveness regarding their work, as they perceive any involvement of others as a personal shortcoming if they do not undertake all tasks unaided. This, indeed, proves to be detrimental to the overall productivity. Having a tendency to exhibit a possessive attitude towards your work significantly decreases your chances of being considered for promotion. You exhibit strong possessiveness over your assigned areas, which is not well-received by upper management. I had the opportunity to peruse an interview featuring esteemed entrepreneur, Richard Branson, wherein he was queried regarding this particular facet of employment. He expressed the notion that retaining positions solely for the purpose of receiving recognition becomes illogical when one chooses to surround oneself with accomplished individuals who are capable of accomplishing tasks more expeditiously. Indeed, the prosperity of his empire would have been significantly compromised had he opted for such a course of action. He remarked that the act of delegation demonstrates confidence in individuals, allowing for the delegation of more significant tasks, resulting in the overall growth and prosperity of the business, benefiting all parties involved.

Email inquiries - In the event that you encounter an email that requires a substantial effort to respond to, please assess whether there exists an individual possessing superior expertise to handle the correspondence. If an opportunity arises, assign the task to another individual, as their ability to expedite the process can lead to more favorable outcomes. The individual whom you entrust with the task will likely exhibit greater efficiency in its completion, while also perceiving your delegation as a demonstration of confidence in their abilities. This quality is highly admirable in a managerial role. By relinquishing possessiveness and adopting a collaborative approach, you demonstrate to management that you do not perceive sharing as a potential threat to your livelihood. Furthermore, this demonstrates to them that you are actively striving towards becoming eligible for a managerial position.

Educating others - Frequently, we are assigned tasks that consume our time but lack stimulation. Frequently, there are subordinate employees who are eagerly anticipating the chance to progress. If you impart the knowledge of handling commonplace matters to these younger individuals, you will observe that they exhibit positive receptiveness due to their acquisition of novel skills. Although filing papers may not be particularly enjoyable, if you elucidate the purpose of the filing process and emphasize its true significance, individuals may perceive it as an expression of trust, indicating that you are delegating them with a responsibility typically reserved for yourself. By imparting knowledge to others, you not only liberate yourself but also cultivate a sense of motivation in your subordinates to actively assist you in accomplishing daily tasks.

Telephone conversations – Similar to the delegation of other tasks, avoid developing a possessive attitude towards your phone calls. In the event that you receive a phone call from an individual seeking assistance beyond your level of expertise, promptly offer your assistance in redirecting them to a more proficient contact rather than causing frustration due to your lack of knowledge. Engaging in a professional approach allows for prioritizing more significant tasks and responsibilities. Please bear in mind that when you have designated a specific time for attending to your phone calls, it is necessary to review your voicemail and reach out to individuals who have attempted to contact you. By adhering to proper conduct and maintaining a courteous and professional demeanor, while ensuring minimal personal phone usage during work hours, your productivity levels will significantly increase. It is imperative to bear in mind that phone contacts can be crucial prospects, therefore, it is essential to diligently record their name and contact details in order to follow up with them if your company develops any offerings that you deem valuable to their needs. Customers are valuable. Don't lose leads.

Convenings - It is plausible that your schedule is quite occupied, causing you to be unable to participate in a gathering. If you happen to be unable to attend, kindly inquire with your supervisor regarding the possibility of delegating note-taking responsibilities to a representative from your department. In this manner, you are able to enjoy the advantages of both options. You will have access to the meeting proceedings while also being afforded additional time to attend to other matters. Utilizing delegation demonstrates confidence in the abilities of subordinates, and they will greatly appreciate the opportunity to undertake such a significant task.

Delegation does not imply the utilization of individuals. It does not signify delegating responsibilities that should rightfully be performed by oneself to others. What it signifies is the equitable distribution of responsibilities, ensuring that all parties reap the advantages of such distribution. Examine the following criteria:

- The response time for customers is expedited.

- The department you are employed in acquires time.

- The task is expedited • The job is completed more rapidly • The work is accomplished at a faster pace

- As an individual acquires knowledge, you consequently derive benefits.

Under no circumstances should one commit the error of unloading unwanted tasks onto another individual, as such behavior does not align with the intended objective. Delegation demonstrates recognition that another individual is better equipped to handle the current task or that their involvement would allow for the prioritization of more urgent matters. Engaging in one-sided relationships where individuals are exploited without receiving any reciprocal benefits, such as knowledge acquisition, does not align with the principle of delegation. It is using people.

Call to Action

Please document the obligations that are to be personally undertaken, as well as those that may be allocated to others. Please allocate the tasks that you must delegate to other individuals. Incorporate the tasks that are within your capability into your schedule.

What Constitutes Significance And Priority?

When considering a list of tasks that need to be completed, there exists a highly efficient approach for establishing priorities, namely, by assigning labels to each individual task. Is your task important? Is your task urgent? Alternatively, is your task of both immediate and significant importance? Finally, is your task devoid of both urgency and importance? Individuals who possess effective time management abilities make it their priority to focus on tasks that are essential to complete, while simultaneously avoiding those that are urgent but not of utmost importance. In relation to our priorities, our aim is to minimize the number of tasks that are both urgent and important, as they tend to perplexingly contribute to undue stress. An imperative I would like to emphasize at this moment is to commence important tasks in advance, refrain from indulging in procrastination, and endeavor to finish them before they reach a point where they become concurrently urgent and significant endeavors. Efficiently engaging in this practice is characteristic of individuals who are highly productive, resulting in a reduction in the overall level of stress they undergo. If you perceive yourself as an individual who tends to closely oversee every aspect that comes their way, including even the minutest tasks or details, you might discover yourself assuming tasks that are pressing in nature but lack significant importance. Instances of this encompass responding to the queries and challenges posed by colleagues via email. Although these tasks may be deemed less significant when compared to larger projects, their urgency surpasses that of the aforementioned endeavors. If one perceives themselves as an individual who acquiesces to all requests and assumes an excessive workload, the ensuing situation may pose challenges for all stakeholders in the professional setting. Engaging in time-sensitive yet nonessential tasks can potentially contribute to an additional degree of avoidable stress. The fundamental argument is that when there is a substantial workload to complete within a restricted timeframe, it is highly probable that the resulting content will be of subpar quality. You could potentially acquire an unfavorable reputation due to the delivery of substandard hastily completed assignments. One possible course of action is to acquire the ability to politely decline the task while conveying a positive disposition to the individual. It entails the skill of refusing supplementary tasks while preserving cordial relationships with colleagues. Expressing a similar sentiment with a formal tone, you could say: "Allow me to convey my desire to assist you; however, I must regretfully inform you that my current time constraints prevent me from executing this task to the desired standard of quality. I hope you understand that my intention is to support my colleagues and not offend." If you encounter situations where individuals rely on your assistance, clarification, or to carry the majority of the workload, such as in the context of delivering a presentation, it is beneficial to cultivate the ability to think and respond swiftly, demonstrating increased spontaneity in your actions. Over time, you will reap greater benefits from this.

Results & Progress

When it comes to time management, the focus should not be on becoming occupied, but rather on achieving progress and generating results consistently throughout each working day. It is advisable to prioritize the delivery of work that is of superior quality, rather than focusing solely on increasing the quantity. Therefore, it is not recommended to unnecessarily fill your schedule with additional tasks in pursuit of a false sense of fulfillment or busyness. Tony Robins espouses the notion that the most effective approach to achieve enduring happiness and a sense of contentment is to consistently strive for advancement in one's professional endeavors and, more fundamentally, one's aspirations. Engaging in tasks such as responding to insignificant or low priority emails throughout the entire day would not yield substantial progress within the given duration. To a certain extent, their significance may be acknowledged, however, in what manner will they cultivate or enhance the progress of your business? If you perceive emails as imperative and time-sensitive in the context of your business operations, it might be opportune to establish a dedicated timeframe each day for addressing and responding to these correspondences. Ideally, I would arrange for a maximum of two time slots per day to accomplish this task - one at noon and the other toward the end of the day. Do not allocate an excessive amount of time to replying to emails unnecessarily. In the majority of instances, such activities are unlikely to yield significant benefits for you, and if they do, it would be advisable to explore means of automating this particular aspect of the business, thereby obviating the need for continual focus on it. Although the notion of extending one's work hours may initially appear favorable, if it merely results in remaining occupied without making substantial advancements, it will have negligible impact on both personal satisfaction and professional growth.

Take A Lunch Break

Numerous individuals who are occupied can be observed persistently toiling during their midday break; however, as per Emma Donaldson-Fielder's counsel, engaging in this practice can prove counterproductive. By engaging in a midday pause of 30 to 60 minutes, individuals are afforded the opportunity to replenish their energy levels and revitalize themselves. This does not imply simply pausing beside your computer desk; ideally, one should relocate oneself from the designated working area. This approach ensures that your mind perceives a genuine break, as taking a temporary leave from your workplace could prove more beneficial than simply resting at your desk. The purpose of taking a lunch break is not to evade additional tasks or to be idle, but conversely, to enable efficient and optimal execution of work in the afternoon.

Merely engage in a thirty-minute walk or partake in a discussion with colleagues, or alternatively arrange a lunch outing with your spouse or a friend. Upon returning to your workstation, you will find yourself reinvigorated and prepared to confront the remaining tasks of the day. One additional advantage of planning is its ability to divide the day into more manageable segments Breaking up those large tasks into smaller pieces will make you more productive because you register these as smaller, simpler and more manageable tasks. Should you choose not to divide tasks in this manner, it will become apparent that there is a substantial project on your agenda, and you may perceive it as a singular, overwhelming task that must be accomplished in one uninterrupted effort. This approach hampers your progress and frequently results in procrastination, thereby jeopardizing the timely completion of significant tasks that fall under the high-stress category of urgent and important.

Step 5: Get Organized

Lack of organization results in ineffective time management as it necessitates the expenditure of valuable time in the quest for essential tools or documents amidst a disarray of disorder. Observing a disorganized workstation may engender a sense of having an abundant workload, leading one to circumvent their tasks.

Although it is indeed factual that one may possess goals, a time plan, a priority list, and a time schedule, it is important to note that the absence of organizational skills may hinder the ease of achieving said goals. By establishing an efficient layout for your workspace (e. In a conducive environment such as a dedicated study area or a well-equipped office, one is able to operate with optimal efficiency without succumbing to overwhelming pressures.

Strategies for Organizing Your Work Space

In order to organize your workspace, employ the subsequent procedure:

Procure three containers and categorize them as 'retain, discard, and donate.' Proceed to deposit into the 'retain' container the articles that are essential and will be utilized during the execution of your engagements or endeavors. In the designated receptacle labeled as the "donation and gifting repository," kindly deposit any possessions that are deemed redundant, yet still possess monetary worth, the potential for charitable contribution, or the possibility of being presented as thoughtful tokens to individuals within your social circle. Finally, place the remaining items that are neither useful nor of value in the "discard" box, and proceed to donate or dispose of these items. This category may encompass damaged kitchenware, torn literature, and similar belongings. Discard these items immediately.

What course of action would you recommend pursuing? That will be covered in the subsequent chapter.

Proceed to Step 6: Establish a Time Management Strategy

Devise a detailed blueprint encompassing the allocation of time for each successive second, minute, and hour of your day. Your time management strategy will be contingent upon your preferred work style, the optimal time of day for addressing specific activities or tasks, and the most conducive environment for task completion. In order to organize your day effectively, it is necessary to engage in advance planning of your activities or tasks.

There are several crucial factors that necessitate your attention during the preliminary planning phase of your activities or tasks.

Establish a Preemptive Daily Schedule: Prior to retiring for the night, it is imperative to meticulously outline and organize your forthcoming day's itinerary by specifying the various activities or tasks you intend to pursue. Please record your daily endeavors, beginning with the utmost priority ones. Dedicate the appropriate amount of time to each task or activity, and ensure you have all the necessary resources prepared in advance to successfully accomplish each of them.

If you allocate a significant amount of time to the selection of your attire, it is advisable to arrange your garments prior to retiring for the night. By doing so, in the morning you will avoid the inefficiency of deliberating on which tasks to prioritize, what attire to select, or what to exclude from your agenda.

Do not succumb to feelings of overwhelm, regardless of the length of your activity list or the apparent busyness of your upcoming day. Alternatively, formulate a structured agenda for your day; strategize the approach for each undertaking, allocate specific time slots for every endeavor, and bear in mind the significance of accomplishing each task on your roster, as well as the subsequent rewards or advantages derived from their completion. By the conclusion of each day or week, you will have successfully attained your predetermined objectives without voicing any grievances regarding the workload endured.

Rise early: Commence your day at an early hour; while waking up early may present a challenge, endeavor to do so. Establish an alarm and ensure its recurring activation nightly. Rising early will provide you with an opportunity to adequately prepare yourself mentally and physically.

Rising early in the morning equips your mind for the forthcoming day's tasks and permits you sufficient time to accomplish your morning regimen prior to commencing your intended duties or engagements. The chaotic nature of the morning rush can instill a sense of bewilderment, thereby setting the stage for a day filled with confusion and stress. Moreover, in the event that you were unable to prioritize and schedule your tasks the previous evening, you can accomplish this in the morning by arising early.

Prioritize Adequate Rest: At times, achieving sound sleep necessitates making certain concessions, such as foregoing a beloved television program, abstaining from internet usage, or refraining from late-night conversations with acquaintances. In order to ensure the effectiveness of the time management process, it is essential to undertake these necessary trade-offs. What strategies can be employed to rise early in the morning despite having slept late? It may be feasible, however, you will experience fatigue throughout the duration of the day.

It is essential for both your physical and mental well-being to engage in relaxation and mental preparation in order to be ready for the activities of the subsequent day. By ensuring adequate rest for your body, you will enhance your ability to focus on activities, thereby minimizing the likelihood of experiencing daytime somnolence.

Document the Persistent Annoyance or Assignment: There exists consistently one matter that has been causing you vexation for an extended duration of days or weeks. Record it daily as you formulate your plan, without omission, even when faced with difficulties or uncertainty, ensuring that you persist until it is accomplished.

It is highly improbable that you will abstain from addressing or resolving your persisting issues or tasks for an extended duration of weeks, or possibly even months. Each instance of revisiting your plan will serve as a reminder to conduct thorough research and ultimately address the task at hand.

In the subsequent phase, we shall acquire the knowledge necessary to organize and allocate your time in a manner that ensures efficient time management.

3. The correlation between physical fitness, well-being, and its impact on individual productivity

Enhancing productivity extends well beyond the confines of the workplace, and a dearth of physical activity can be correlated with decreased levels of productivity. Engaging in consistent physical activity and maintaining a nutritious eating regimen will enhance one's overall well-being, elevate levels of vitality, and promote enhanced cognitive clarity and concentration.

Herein, I present a series of measures that you may undertake to enhance physical well-being and elevate levels of productivity within a designated period:

Incorporate brief intervals of physical activity into your daily routine: Endeavor to allocate a minimum of 3-5 minutes within each hour to engage in exercise, such as brisk walking or performing squats. Please consider engaging in activities that enable you to multitask with a few less demanding tasks simultaneously. You could, for instance, engage in tasks such as reviewing emails, responding to phone calls, or engaging in comparable activities. Incorporating brief bouts of physical activity throughout the day renders it more feasible, and engaging in simultaneous tasks enhances your productivity and bestows a heightened feeling of accomplishment.

Establish an exercise regimen, adhere to a fitness podcast, and COMMUNICATE: Determine a structured exercise schedule along with specific time slots allocated for physical activity. To facilitate your progress, seek out a podcast that brings you pleasure. There exists a plethora of complimentary fitness podcasts at your disposal, which can be accessed and utilized at your convenience. Even in the form of recorded guidance, these podcasts will provide assistance throughout your fitness journey. Additionally, it is advisable to communicate your objectives with another individual. It proves advantageous to have an individual readily available, who can assume the role of an accountability partner, thereby offering assistance in terms of motivation and ensuring adherence to set objectives.

Enhance your hydration habits and adopt a more nutritious diet: This advice may seem commonplace, yet it remains crucial; prioritize proper hydration and mindfully consider the quality of your food. You will be astonished by the significant impact that incremental modifications to your dietary habits can achieve as well. One can gradually decrease the quantity of sugar present in their beverages, consume an increased amount of vegetables, and choose baked alternatives over fried food, among other measures. In addition to enhancing overall health and well-being, these activities contribute to improved metabolic function, heightened levels of energy, and facilitate enhanced concentration, thereby promoting increased productivity within shorter time spans.

Allocate time for rest and rejuvenation: It is essential that you carve out a portion of your schedule to engage in moments of rest and relaxation. This entails not excessively indulging in sleep, but rather obtaining an appropriate duration of rest as necessary, while also taking breaks from work-related engagements. Engaging in this practice will facilitate an optimal state of physical and mental well-being, enabling you to undertake your responsibilities with unwavering concentration and utmost proficiency.

Efficient Strategies For Time Management

It is inherently discernible whether an individual possesses proficient time management skills or not. If one consistently exemplifies punctuality and timeliness in the completion of their responsibilities, it is likely attributable to their adeptness in effectively managing their time. In the event that you consistently exhibit tardiness, it would be prudent for you to consider acquiring time management instruction and guidance. It is crucial for each individual to acquire the ability to complete tasks within the designated timeframe, regardless of the workload at hand. The manner in which one handles and organizes their time holds significant weight, as it directly impacts the timely and successful completion of tasks. Provided below are several invaluable strategies and techniques for effective time management, aiding in the improvement of one's ability to efficiently allocate and utilize their time.

Devise a daily schedule.

It is necessary to establish a daily itinerary in advance. This is the sole means by which you will comprehend the necessary tasks to engage in during specific periods of the day, thereby preventing aimless loitering and the consequent squandering of time. Many individuals strategically prepare for their day either the previous evening or during the early hours of the morning, which is an opportune moment. Having a well-structured plan allows you to anticipate the course of your day prior to its actual commencement. Throughout the course of the day, your primary objective is to adhere to the plan to the greatest extent feasible. If an unforeseen circumstance arises during the course of the day, it becomes conveniently feasible to adjust the plan accordingly.

Get an organizer

In order to consistently remain informed and well-prepared, it is imperative to possess an implement for managing and coordinating tasks and responsibilities, commonly referred to as an organizer. Many individuals will fail to achieve significant accomplishments if they have not properly structured their lives. It is essential to effectively structure your to-do lists, projects, and any significant matters that may arise in life. Utilizing an organizer facilitates a clear distinction between completed and pending tasks, enabling you to ascertain the remaining actions required to fulfill a specific task.

Give a time limit for each task of the day

It is imperative to strategize the allotted time required for completing a given task. Establishing incremental deadlines is crucial in ensuring the timely completion of all tasks by the day's end. By following this approach, you will be able to avoid the temptation of wasting time in between tasks, as doing so would result in the incomplete execution of a specific task by the end of the day. Additionally, this will guarantee that no task is monopolizing the time allotted for other tasks.

Acquire the ability to decline

Many individuals undertake an excessive workload that surpasses their capacity, resulting in heightened levels of stress due to insufficient time to complete all tasks. Many individuals permit others to consume a significant portion of their time, thereby neglecting the pursuit of their daily objectives. One must develop the ability to decline or refuse commitments beyond one's capacity, in order to effectively manage their workload. Resist all forms of distractions and temptations as well. If feasible, reschedule the distractions to a future date in order to devote your attention to your current tasks.

Please ensure that you have your time schedule in your possession.

It is imperative that you carry your daily schedule with you consistently. Utilizing a calendar proves to be a straightforward endeavor, particularly when you seamlessly synchronize it with your mobile device, thereby granting you constant awareness of your obligations and tasks. Having such a closely packed schedule would prevent you from squandering time on less essential tasks when you have already assigned significance to another engagement on the same day.

It is advisable to commence your day at an early hour.

It will be highly improbable for you to adhere to your schedule if you consistently commence your day behind schedule. The ultimate undesired outcome is to be tardy, thus it is crucial to commence promptly. If, for example, you have a scheduled appointment, make an effort to arrive early to avoid being tardy. In order to ensure promptness and preparedness for your work tasks, it is advisable to arrive ahead of schedule and meticulously strategize your agenda prior to commencing your work duties. It is recommended that you submit your contributions in advance, thus allowing ample time to accommodate any potential revisions or modifications required before the final submission deadline.

Place significance on meeting your deadlines.

Deadlines represent the predetermined moments by which completion of tasks is expected. It is imperative that these matters are highlighted to convey their gravity and to ensure that you refrain from engaging with them carelessly. It is imperative that the deadlines are explicitly defined. Make note of them on your calendar and meticulously prepare, ensuring that you familiarize yourself with them thoroughly prior to commencing your day.

Ensure that you always have a watch or a clock within proximity

When endeavoring to effectively allocate time amidst various tasks, it is of paramount importance to refrain from inadvertently losing track of time. It is inadvisable to allocate excessive time to a single task to the detriment of others. Hence, it is imperative to effectively manage one's time in order to sufficiently allocate the necessary amount of time to each task, resulting in favorable outcomes. You need to be aware of time at all times, which is why you need a good watch or clock placed strategically to where you are working from so that you can constantly see how much time you have left to finish that task.

Abstain from any source of diversion

External stimuli can hinder one's concentration, which is crucial when endeavoring to meet a time constraint. It is imperative to discern the various factors that impede your efficacy in order to eliminate them entirely. Certain distractions that necessitate your attention include incoming messages on the phone, phone calls, individuals entering and exiting the office, a coworker who frequently engages in lengthy conversations during working hours, and similar interruptions. Please disable your chat applications and restrict their usage to break times or post-work hours. Disassociate yourself from individuals who impede your ability to work with optimal efficiency. Please power down your mobile device if you continue to receive personal calls and are unable to maintain focus on your work tasks.

Exploring Strategies To Implement Your Objectives

Formal alternative: "Establishing goals may be deemed straightforward, yet executing them remains an integral aspect within the larger context." One can engage in extensive planning and diligently document their goals; however, unless decisive measures are undertaken, no progress will be achieved. Individuals who are consistently occupied occasionally refrain from undertaking tasks due to the perception of lacking the necessary time or energy to do so. Nevertheless, it is an uncomplicated approach to achieve your objectives by integrating your minor goals into your daily routine. When formulating an objective, one should not anticipate its instantaneous attainment. Efforts exerted over a considerable period and with substantial energy are integral to the process of striving towards and actualizing one's objectives.

Do you have aspirations that often remain confined to the planning phase? Have you considered strategies that can be employed to integrate your goals within the context of your life? The subsequent course of action entails translating your objectives into concrete outcomes. In the forthcoming chapter, we will explore strategies that facilitate the gradual implementation of your objectives, enabling you to avoid any overwhelming sensations.

Commence by laying the foundation

Upon determining a collection of objectives that you intend to actively strive towards, it is necessary to commence from the initial stage. Should you attempt to tackle the more challenging tasks at the outset, you will likely experience heightened frustration and a diminished resolve to persevere towards your objective. Allocate a sufficient amount of time to determine the most appropriate starting point and proceed through the procedure incrementally. When pursuing a goal, it is crucial to initiate action, even if the beginning is modest in scale.

Begin with Incremental Objectives and Progress towards Loftier Objectives

When considering the realm of goal setting, you will discover that certain objectives will possess a greater magnitude compared to others. Upon examination of these objectives, ascertain those that can be managed at a more modest scale and gradually progress from that point. Once you have acquired the proficiency in implementing objectives, you will ascertain how to effectively address more substantial aspirations and manifest them into actuality. Acquiring proficiency in managing the smaller objectives will serve as a solid foundation for addressing the larger aspirations.

Prioritize Your Goals

Some of the objectives that you establish will hold greater relevance to your current life circumstances and professional trajectory. Several of these aspirations may currently appear as mere fanciful wishes, yet they hold potential for more substantial fulfillment in the times ahead. Consider prioritizing specific objectives while temporarily deferring others until you deem yourself sufficiently prepared and capable to dedicate your complete focus to them. Certain individuals often find themselves burdened with an excessive number of goals that they aspire to pursue concurrently, resulting in a state of overwhelming stress, ultimately impeding any substantive progress towards achieving said goals.

Do not overwhelm yourself by assuming excessive responsibilities simultaneously.

Individuals who are occupied with various responsibilities often assume a workload that surpasses their capacity to manage effectively. Although individuals may find enjoyment in being occupied, the burden of assuming additional tasks can induce anxiety and result in a diversion of attention from genuine priorities. Exercise caution by conscientiously recognizing your boundaries and behaving in alignment with them. In case you discover that your schedule is overly packed, it is advisable to pause and redirect your attention towards prioritizing tasks that are essential for successfully achieving your objectives.

Engage the assistance of another individual in order to uphold your accountability

Employing the services of an individual who can assume the responsibility of holding you accountable for your objectives constitutes an alternative approach that ensures your ongoing commitment to their attainment, thereby preventing their neglect. Ensuring that someone inquires about your progress and your level of commitment towards your goals enables you to consistently prioritize them and devise strategies to pursue them, even during periods of overwhelming busyness. Individuals with demanding schedules tend to prioritize immediate tasks instead of considering the ultimate objective. Therefore, enlisting assistance from a companion can be instrumental in maintaining one's concentration, enabling a determined endeavor to guarantee the realization of the desired goal.

"Do not let obstacles serve as a source of discouragement.

Life is replete with an array of challenges and impediments. If we permit the presence of these obstacles to impede our progress, achieving the ultimate goal would be rendered unattainable. When confronted with adversities in life, strive to confront them directly and persevere until triumph is achieved, overcoming obstacles and progressing towards the desired outcome. Individuals who do not possess considerable strength are susceptible to allowing such obstacles to cause distress. However, acquiring the capacity to effectively deal with unforeseen challenges and impediments will facilitate personal growth and enable progress towards the realization of one's aspirations.

Initiating progress towards achieving your goals can be exceedingly daunting and challenging. By examining your mindset and devising strategies to initiate and sustain progress, you can enhance your prospects for achieving success in the objectives you establish for both your personal development and professional trajectory. Indeed, there are certain unforeseen circumstances in life that may impede the timely attainment of these objectives; nevertheless, persevere in making progressive efforts towards realizing the ultimate vision.

Establishing Deadlines For Your Assignments

One might contemplate this query when they have expended valuable time without achieving any significant outcomes. One factor contributing to your tendency to engage in procrastination and time wastage rather than promptly initiating action is your inability to establish clear and predetermined deadlines for your tasks.

Indeed, a task lacking a specified deadline remains unfinished. The absence of a designated timeframe for a task tends to foster procrastination, as it creates a perception of having an unrestricted amount of time to accomplish the chore.

In order to prevent the onset of procrastination and ensure the timely accomplishment of tasks, it is imperative to assign a specific deadline to each task. This process transforms a task into a quantifiable one, allowing individuals to assess their performance upon task completion. An example of this would be that setting a goal to "compose a speech for the upcoming seminar by Friday" can be considered measurable, as opposed to simply setting a goal to "write a speech," since the latter lacks a means of measuring your progress or determining if the task has been accomplished.

Herein lies a methodology for establishing practical time constraints for your assignments and dutifully executing your customary operational strategies.

Initial Step: Acquire Knowledge of the Time Constraints

When scrutinizing the particulars of a given task, ascertain the deadline for its completion. What is the expected duration for the completion of this task and by when is it required? On occasion, individuals of higher hierarchical status, such as one's superior at the workplace, may explicitly articulate a definitive time limit.

Typically, though, you possess the opportunity to select a specific timeframe for a given task. For example, in the event that you make the decision to introduce a novel product for your organization, you possess the opportunity to determine the timing of its release.

In order to establish a deadline for such tasks, carefully analyze each intricate aspect of the task to determine the necessary amount of time for its successful completion. Exercise rationality and establish a suitable time frame for each task. In the event that a task proves exceedingly challenging and necessitates extensive research, it is advisable to allocate several weeks or even a month to successfully accomplish it.

Once you have determined the deadline, be sure to record it in your calendar and organizer to ensure that you do not overlook it.

Second Step: Establish Time Constraints for Your Assignments.

Once you have established a deadline, proceed to delineate the various incremental tasks necessary for the successful completion of the overarching objective. Assign a specific timeframe to each of these constituent parts, ensuring a structured and efficient progression. If your intention is to commence the introduction of the new product precisely in a span of two months, I kindly request your estimation regarding the duration necessary for activities such as product research, manufacturing, vendor selection, marketing, and additional related endeavors.

Consider all of these factors and establish deadlines for each subordinate task associated with a major objective. This will assist you in preventing your tasks from impeding or consuming time allocated for other pursuits.

Proceed to Step 3: Employing Calendars and Organizers

One fundamental and highly advantageous method for organizing your regular tasks is by employing a calendar. Utilize Google Calendar or any alternative electronic calendar on your personal computer, in addition to a physical calendar as well. Please designate the various tasks you have resolved to accomplish on a specific day and week by marking them on the calendar.

It is advisable to synchronize the Google Calendar on your computer with the one on your mobile phone or any other device you frequently utilize, ensuring convenient access to your regular schedule from anywhere you may be. In addition, make use of the assistance provided by an organizer. It is essential to diligently arrange and manage all pertinent information, projects, task registers, and miscellaneous artifacts.

Fourth step: Employ a whiteboard-based calendaring system

Another option available is to construct a customized whiteboard calendar. A whiteboard calendar serves as a highly effective tool for monitoring and documenting one's tasks as well as the overall progress achieved. Obtain a whiteboard, and employ dry erase markers to illustrate a calendar that can be modified on a monthly basis. Create columns for tasks that cannot be altered: tasks that must be carried out regularly, tasks that are prone to change, tasks that are currently in progress, and tasks that have been completed.

Please include the various tasks you intend to complete within these categories, noting their nature with a distinct marker for each task type. As an example, a task that cannot be altered may be denoted using a red marker, whereas completed tasks may be indicated using green or similar markers.

This simplifies the process of inputting various tasks onto the calendar, resulting in an organized and more manageable system. To update a task or modify its status, you simply need to remove it from its previous category and replace it with the new category in the corresponding column, using the designated color. Once you have finished the task of 'laundry,' you may place it in the 'accomplished' section, denoted by the color green.

The utilization of the interchangeable marker technique facilitates the seamless modification of task statuses and allows for convenient updates to be made to your calendar. Please ensure to update your calendar each evening prior to retiring for the night and each morning upon awakening. It is advisable to position the calendar within accessible locations such as the kitchen, bedroom, or any other frequented area, as this practice aids in effectively managing one's action plan and mitigates the chances of overlooking crucial tasks.

Step 5: Consistently Refer to Your Planner on a Daily Basis

Upon establishing deadlines and schedules for your tasks and incorporating them into your calendar and organizer, make it a habit to review your planner, calendar, whiteboard calendar, or organizer - whichever medium you are utilizing - each morning promptly after awakening.

Ensure that you establish an alarm or a reminder to prompt you to examine your planner promptly upon awakening, so as to avoid forgetting. Engaging in this routine for a few successive days will help solidify this behavior as a habit, ultimately leading you to develop the regular practice of consulting your planner every morning upon waking up. This will guarantee perpetual awareness of your scheduled tasks for each day.

Having acknowledged this, it can occasionally pose a challenge to initiate the implementation of your action plan. Despite repeatedly checking and scrutinizing your calendar in the morning, you persistently defer your tasks and fail to promptly address them. This occurrence arises as a result of your deeply rooted tendency to engage in procrastination.

In order to become an adept time manager, it is imperative to conquer procrastination. The subsequent chapter extensively addresses this matter and imparts strategies on how to permanently surmount procrastination.

The Significance Of A Task List For Achieving Short-Term And Long-Term Objectives

Upon recognizing that you are the sole possessor of the key that unlocks the gateway to embarking on your path towards success and fulfillment, your subsequent course of action should involve strategic planning. Similar to the diligent preparation of a dutiful soldier prior to engaging in battle, it is imperative that you commit your thoughts and plans onto parchment. Develop a strategic design for both your short-term and long-term objectives, carefully consider your actions, and eliminate any superfluous steps that may hinder the effectiveness of your plan during the organizational process.

If you harbor any doubts or believe that you might have unwittingly overlooked something, it would be advisable to seek the counsel of a confidant or a cherished companion. They will be the appropriate selection due to the high likelihood of your significant level of trust in them. Kindly ask them to verify the list on your behalf and, if needed, include any additional ideas or goals. By doing so, you will widen the scope of your opportunities. They are also capable of acquainting you with prior experiences they have undergone. It is important to bear in mind that collaboration and the combination of ideas can lead to superior outcomes, as the collective intelligence of multiple individuals is often more advantageous than that of a single person. It is more advisable to seek the assistance of a loved one whenever you are faced with the task of making a life-altering decision.

While you may believe that creating to-do lists is unnecessary and that you have a clear understanding of your priorities, the truth contradicts this assumption. Researchers have demonstrated that the utilization of task lists is a validated strategy for nurturing motivation and significantly enhancing individuals' goal achievement.

A research conducted on individuals with cardiac conditions spanning a decade exposed that nearly half of the subjects relapse into unhealthy habits within a few months despite their prior experience of heart disease. Among the 50% who quickly return to their previous lifestyle, the primary observation indicates that none of them make efforts to fortify their convictions regarding a healthy way of life. Individuals who successfully eliminated detrimental behaviors such as smoking, excessive drinking, and consuming unhealthy foods implemented a practice of documenting their tasks and other important information, and consistently endeavored to strengthen their mindset on a daily basis.

By utilizing basic cues and memory prompts, they managed to abstain from the deleterious behaviors stemming from their compromised well-being. The remaining individuals, despite facing significant challenges, were unable to accomplish the task due to a deficiency in agents enforcing proper conduct.

It is imperative that you systematically identify and document the tasks that are necessary for you to undertake. It is not mandatory for it to be a to-do list (opt for any approach that suits your needs), but ensure consistent dedication to the routine until it becomes ingrained in your behavior.

Please refrain from delaying attending to this matter. Kindly cease perusing the book and set aside your iPad, computer, and smartphone in order to commence taking notes promptly.

Please regard this as a gentle reminder and proceed with your tasks promptly. I will be meeting you shortly.

Achieving Proficiency In A Time Management System

Attaining proficiency in the art of time optimization forms the fundamental basis for asserting command over one's own time. This skill empowers individuals to effectively manage their time, thereby enabling them to regain control over their lives. According to popular belief, failure to pursue one's own aspirations may result in being enlisted by others to manifest their own ambitions.

The initial action towards achieving your aspirations involves reestablishing command over your time. Therefore, allow me to present a time optimization system that will efficiently steer you on the path ahead.

The aforementioned system utilizes a blend of external resourcing, prioritizing prompt task completion, cultivating intense concentration, and eradicating any potential diversions.

Despite the system being replete with substantial advantages, The Time Optimization System is remarkably uncomplicated and readily applicable, comprising a set of five sequential steps.

Applying the Initial Principle of Time

First, monitor the amount of time allocated to each specific task.

- By discerning the exact amount of time allocated to each task within your workflow, you will be able to obtain a comprehensive understanding of the manner in which you allocate your daily schedule. This could potentially be the initial instance where you have conscientiously examined your actions and meticulously analyzed them on a per-minute basis. Examining the choices and deeds undertaken over the course of one's life inevitably unveils an individual's personal blueprint for existence.

Proceed to the second step: Determine favorable time slots in your schedule to allocate additional time.

- This step is straightforward yet quite impressive. - The simplicity of this step is surpassed only by its impressive nature. - Although this step may appear simplistic, it is undeniably impressive. - Despite its simple nature, this step is remarkably cool. - This step is characterized by its simplicity, which makes it particularly cool. Seek out the readily available opportunities that exist for you to create more time within the confines of your professional schedule. Create a strategic plan outlining your proposed course of actions, and commence the process of systematizing and consolidating said actions in a more methodical and structured fashion. The greater amount of time you devote to a particular subject within a consolidated period, the more rapidly you become proficient in that sequence of activities.

- An alternative approach to identifying opportunities involves exploring innovative methods to enhance productivity and expedite workflow. Please consider reviewing the instances in which you have taken breaks and engaged in distractions such as checking emails or engaging in conversations with colleagues. An effective means of enhancing productivity during the work day is by maintaining uninterrupted concentration. Implementing uninfluenced actions significantly enhances daily productivity by a factor of five.

Step 3: Develop solutions for each identified opportunity.

Engage in a 15-minute ideation session to devise strategies for efficiently accomplishing daily and weekly objectives. Step 2 provided several guidelines and techniques for generating solutions to enhance time availability, yet you possess the ultimate knowledge of the most effective means to optimize your time. Please bear in mind that it is possible to delegate a significant portion of the straightforward tasks to external parties, and also that you may choose to restrict access to your email and physically isolate yourself in the office during specific time periods. This will significantly enhance your productivity.

-Additional options encompass the engagement of a domestic laborer for weekly cleaning of your dwelling or alternatively, striving to accomplish dishwashing within a three-minute timeframe and subsequently tidying the kitchen within a span of ten minutes. Regardless of whether you opt for outsourcing tasks or personally undertaking them, it is imperative to determine the extent of time saved by actively pushing yourself to complete tasks expeditiously.

Step 4: Implement three strategies that yield expedited outcomes.

- Once you have concluded the process of generating ideas to allocate more time in your daily routine, select the three solutions that promptly yield time-saving benefits and implement them. This will promptly provide recompense for your deliberate efforts to create more spare time and enhance your life. Through observing swift outcomes, you will come to comprehend the efficacy of managing time and harnessing it to your advantage.

Step 5: Utilize the spare time acquired from step four in order to implement the solution that yields the maximum time efficiency. Continue the process until you have exhausted all feasible options to incorporate into your timetable.

- The implementation of Step 4 will inevitably result in a significant amount of newfound free time, which can be regarded as highly favorable. Significant and efficient outcomes within the Time Optimization System are derived from step 5. The aforementioned procedures enabled you to ascertain the allocation of your time and quantify the amount of time that has been liberated as a result of the fourth step. Step 5 uses the free time you made to further free up time and drastically free up your life so you can spend time truly doing the things you love.

- It is a requirement for each solution to allocate a certain amount of time for implementation. - The implementation of every solution necessitates a time investment. - All solutions entail a time commitment for implementation. Utilize the time that has been unoccupied during step 4 to identify a suitable resolution that aligns with the timeframe that has been vacated from the previous step. Select the option that will yield the greatest amount of leisure time upon implementation, and subsequently reevaluate the duration of your free time.

- Iteratively perform this procedure by evaluating your newly allotted time and implementing the optimal solution within the confines of that temporal interval.

- Continue iterating this process until you reach a point where you are no longer able to find additional solutions, either due to depletion of available options or exceeding the designated time frame.

The time optimization system adheres to a sole governing principle:

After step 4 is completed, never exceed your original work time.

Your objective is to conserve time in your work endeavors, not squander it.

A prime example:

The initial three solutions promptly create a surplus of 1.5 hours in your daily schedule. Therefore, it is imperative that the duration of the solution implemented during the 5th step does not surpass the maximum time limit of 1.5 hours. The objective is to ensure that one does not exceed the duration of their original work period prior to implementing the system.

Mitigating Distractions And Time-Consuming Activities

On certain occasions, one may come across situations or individuals that inadvertently or knowingly engage in actions that are designed to consume one's time. Engaging in diversions and activities that consume time can significantly deplete the precious resource of time. By effectively reducing these, you will observe a noticeable increase in the amount of time available to accomplish tasks.

The subsequent recommendations are applicable to both professional and personal domains. By implementing these strategies, you will enhance your time management skills significantly.

Phone

Your mobile device has the capability to greatly impede your focus and productivity during the course of the day, particularly if you are required to remain seated at a workstation for the majority of the time. When you know you are going to be incredibly busy, turn the phone off or onto silent. Restore operation during designated time intervals and provide prior notification of this schedule to others. Enable callers to leave voicemails, and subsequently utilize periods of diminished activity to promptly respond to these messages.

Research findings have indicated that individuals have a higher propensity to limit the duration of their phone conversations when they are in an upright position, as opposed to being seated. Ensure that discussions are concise and focused, refraining from engaging in superfluous casual chatter. If you possess a personal cellular device that you bring to the workplace, it would be advisable not to provide your colleagues or superiors with your contact details. Numbers you ring often should be stored close to your phone so you don't have to go hunting around searching for them.

Email

In the realm of the internet, a significant amount of your daily routine may be dedicated exclusively to the act of inspecting your electronic mail. To mitigate the potential for email-related interruptions, it is recommended to limit the frequency of email checks to a few designated intervals throughout the day.

When not actively monitoring the browser, please ensure to close it and set email notifications to a muted or silent mode. Similar to your phone, it is advisable to establish designated intervals for reviewing and addressing any incoming emails. The presence of a substantial number of unread emails can serve as a hindrance to productivity and lead to heightened levels of stress.

Please expeditiously remove all unsolicited email and any other content that is not pertinent to your needs. If you find yourself unable to address a specific matter due to potential lack of accurate information, it would be advisable to redirect the issue to a more suitable individual and subsequently archive the email in a pertinent folder. Establish directories within your email client that can autonomously categorize incoming emails. Additionally, exercise caution when encountering emails labeled as Urgent or High Priority, as they may not necessarily be of immediate importance.

Mail

There are two primary recommendations regarding handling mail in a formal setting. Firstly, it is advisable to open mail in close proximity to a waste receptacle, discarding any superfluous or unwanted materials. Secondly, promptly attending to and responding to any relevant correspondence is essential.

Computers

Computers provide ample enjoyment but also engender a plethora of interruptions, resulting in notable vexations. Herein lies a compendium of valuable recommendations for effectively managing and mitigating potential disruptions arising from computer-related diversions. Initially, once you have completed your work on an application or file, ensure its closure and subsequent storage. All webpages should be promptly exited, particularly those of social media platforms such as Facebook and Twitter. If possible, consider disabling your Internet connection until your lunch break or in case of necessity.

For individuals who may be inclined to partake in a brief game during intermissions, it is advised to remove the software from the computer. Frequently create backups of your work and ensure the security of your computer by implementing measures against viruses.

Meetings

Conducting meetings is a crucial aspect of business operations, although they have the potential to consume a substantial amount of time. It is advisable to reach a prior consensus regarding the duration of the meetings, considering that individuals typically have other pressing commitments. Please ensure punctuality for the meetings to avoid being tardy or ahead of schedule. In the event of a prolonged duration of the meeting, it would be advisable to kindly request permission to depart as deliberations turn inconsequential to your involvement. Additionally, if feasible, employing a structured agenda with predetermined time allotments could prove instrumental in managing the meeting's length.

Visitors

Efficient management of visitors is an essential aspect of a well-structured life. Coordinate visitor schedules during periods of relatively low activity and limit the duration of each visit or appointment to approximately 10 – 15 minutes. If an individual should arrive unexpectedly and their presence proves inconvenient, it is advisable to kindly express that the current time is not optimal for a visit and endeavor to schedule an alternative date.

Family Commitments

The significance of familial bonds should not be underestimated, as they necessitate a considerable investment of time. Hence, utilize a calendar as a means to record and allocate appointments or activities for each individual on specific dates and times. Ensure that all pertinent documents, including reports, permission slips, and other necessary paperwork, are kept in close proximity to the calendar. Additionally, it is advisable to have readily accessible phone numbers and addresses that may be required. Dispose of said documents once they are deemed unnecessary.

Stress

Do you observe an increase in your stress levels as your list of tasks continues to expand? When we are overwhelmed with tasks, our patience may become strained, resulting in the emergence of irritable dispositions. The experience of stress can lead to increased levels of distraction, as well as negatively impact both one's physical well-being and the emotional state of those in proximity. While experiencing stress is commonplace, it is advisable to endeavor for relaxation and composure. Kindly notify others that your current workload is exceedingly demanding, and express the necessity for uninterrupted time to accomplish pending tasks. You will discover that they possess a considerable degree of empathy, and there exists a possibility that they may offer assistance to you.

Focus

A crucial element in effective time management is maintaining a sense of focus. The greater your concentration on tasks at hand, the more efficiently you are able to utilize your time.

The contemporary era has presented us with various diversions, rendering concentration appear challenging. Nevertheless, it is imperative to maintain constant command. One should assume an active role in determining the course of technology rather than letting technology dictate one's path.

Maintaining a high level of concentration is imperative in the realm of time management and productivity, as it facilitates the assimilation of information, accomplishment of tasks, and optimization of energy levels.

This chapter will address straightforward techniques for reclaiming and sustaining focus.

Quit multi-tasking. Single-task.

In light of the myriad technological advancements, sophisticated tools, and software available today, individuals have become highly proficient in the art of multitasking. Nevertheless, can the act of multitasking truly be regarded as the most efficient approach to time management, or does it merely deplete one's time instead?

An increasing body of evidence indicates that engaging in multiple tasks simultaneously is less effective in comparison to a sequential approach. A recent study has uncovered that individuals engage in multitasking not solely for the purpose of enhancing productivity, but rather due to the satisfaction it provides. The greater the number of tasks completed simultaneously, the more pronounced the sense of fulfillment becomes. However, this practice consistently yields unsatisfactory outcomes.

Research has revealed that the structure of the human brain is fundamentally ill-suited for the task of multitasking. The human brain exhibits the capacity to concurrently attend to multiple stimuli, however, in such instances, the brain undergoes a process of "divisive attention". This phenomenon is commonly referred to by researchers as "spotlights", denoting the exertion of cognitive effort by the brain in transitioning between different activities.

Furthermore, it was discovered that individuals who engage in multitasking display a deterioration in specific abilities, such as their capacity to assimilate information. In conclusion, engaging in multiple tasks simultaneously significantly diminishes productivity.

If you consider yourself a committed practitioner of multi-tasking, it is never too late to disengage from this inclination. Rather than engaging in multi-tasking, focus on the practice of single-tasking.

When operating a computer, the allure of multitasking can be quite strong. An effective strategy to mitigate this behavior involves restricting oneself to using only one tab on each occasion. Rather than maintaining multiple tabs open in your browser, which enables multitasking, cultivate self-discipline and consistently limit yourself to having only one tab open. Rather than engaging in simultaneous activities such as tweeting, checking Facebook, sending an e-mail, reading an article, and watching a YouTube video, it is advisable to focus on completing one task at a time. By adopting this approach, you will be able to channel all of your attention and effort into a solitary undertaking, thereby increasing your overall level of productivity.

In the preceding chapters, you have acquired knowledge regarding the significance of selecting your pivotal tasks (MITs) and prioritizing them to facilitate enhanced productivity and foster effective time management. Engaging in the identification of your

Most Important Tasks (MITs) can be considered a highly effective approach for honing the skill of focusing on a single task at a time.

Once you've chosen your MITs for the day or hour, it is advisable not to do anything else before you accomplish these tasks. In the event that any of your Most Important Tasks does not necessitate the use of a computer, it is advisable to power down your computer to prevent any potential distractions. If your objective is to engage in a writing endeavor, it is advisable to disconnect your Internet connection in order to minimize potential distractions. If preliminary research is necessary for your writing, it is advisable to commence with that task prior to directing your attention towards the actual composition.

Maintain a simplified lifestyle and prioritize singular tasks, as this approach is conducive to achieving higher levels of productivity.

Limit distractions.

Distractions are everywhere. Blaise Pascal once stated, "Distraction is the sole source of solace amidst our sufferings, yet paradoxically, it remains the most significant of our afflictions."

At times, individuals succumb to distractions. Nevertheless, for individuals aspiring to become proficient in time management and consistently maintain high productivity levels, it is advisable to minimize all sources of distraction.

Initially, it is imperative to underscore that certain "distractions" exhibit a subjective nature. The act of being distracted for one individual might engender a state of focused attention for another. For example, certain individuals derive a sense of tranquility and productivity from the presence of ambient music during their work endeavors, whereas others perceive it as an obstacle to optimal performance. Furthermore, certain individuals are able to maintain high levels of productivity despite working in a noisy setting such as a coffee shop, as they perceive a quiet room to be lacking in sufficient stimulation. In the meantime, certain individuals necessitate absolute tranquility in order to accomplish their optimum productivity.

Be cognizant of your personal work habits and the strategies that enhance your productivity, excluding the practice of multitasking, of course. After ensuring the establishment of that, endeavor to eliminate any sources of disruption.

Interruptions from colleagues constitute one of the primary factors contributing to distractions. One traditional yet highly efficient approach to address this matter is to display a DND sign, which stands for Do Not Disturb sign. Place it outside your entrance or in the vicinity of your workspace where it is clearly visible to others. It would be advantageous to inform your colleagues in advance that you require utmost concentration during work. Kindly communicate the specific periods during which you will not be accessible, and kindly request them to contact you via email for any urgent matters, which you can attend to after those designated hours.

3. Remove unnecessary items.

The presence of clutter, although seemingly benign, has been scientifically substantiated to impact an individual's level of productivity. Does the presence of a disorganized setting contribute positively to the enhancement of time management skills, productivity, or does it rather result in an increased amount of time spent searching for items and sifting through extensive piles of belongings?

Removing excess clutter is vital for enhancing productivity. An effective method to overcome clutter is to designate a specific location for each item. For example, it is imperative that incoming paperwork is appropriately organized and that the same level of organization be applied to outgoing documents. All office supplies may be stored in a single drawer, if possible, in an organized manner, while mail can be placed in a separate drawer. Discover an optimal approach that aligns with your needs and preferences.

Develop a regular practice of maintaining an organized and clutter-free work environment. It need not be excessively tidy; rather, it should possess a level of pleasantness that enables you to remain focused and productive.

Learning Time Management

Acquiring proficiency in time management is perceived to be less challenging than commonly believed. Indeed, upon commencing our educational journey, we engage in the acquisition of novel techniques that facilitate the achievement of objectives. As our parents instruct us, we simultaneously acquire crucial time management abilities as well. The benefit of acquiring knowledge necessitates adequate instruction, and given the diverse range of educational opportunities available in our society, this is where the challenge of managing time arises. The most valuable aspect of acquiring knowledge is discovering our true selves. We receive guidance from various sources such as our parents, educational institutions, social circles, political figures, publications, and numerous other outlets, all of which offer diverse perspectives on how to achieve optimal outcomes.

Our parents serve as invaluable educators in life due to their genuine concern for their children's well-being, which enables them to provide clear guidance and help in recognizing and learning from their mistakes. Educators are equally commendable; however, it must be acknowledged that individuals have undergone varying upbringings, a matter which predominantly influences our cognition and conduct. An appropriate approach to time management entails comprehending one's unique attributes and personal limitations. If you are encountering difficulty, it is possible that you are employed in a position that surpasses your capacity to perform effectively as an individual. You may wish to seek employment that aligns with your aptitudes and talents. Attempting to undertake more than one can manage is among the initial stages on the path towards failure. If this assertion is accurate, it would seem that your ability to effectively manage your time is disorganized. It is possible that you are currently falling short of the expectations set for you, but possess the capability to successfully fulfill your duties. Nevertheless, the time management system is disorganized.

Time management can be analyzed based on individual characteristics, although, to a great extent, it entails effectively juggling tasks without impeding workflow or surpassing our capacity to handle them. It is imperative for us to possess the capacity to modify our plans, as individuals, locations, objects, and enterprises undergo transformations. We require a structured hierarchy of competencies to ensure the successful execution of a plan, along with the capacity to adhere to and fulfill said plans. It is imperative that we acquire the ability to embrace changes as they arise, while also developing our aptitude for social skills and adapting our behavioral patterns, thereby effectively managing our time. Modifications are acknowledged through appropriate consequences and incentives. Should we be unable to embrace the changes that life presents, it is possible that the absence of objective consequences may be a contributing factor. When confronted with a challenging situation and responding appropriately, a recognition is expected, yet when faced with adversity and experiencing failure, retribution is expected. Punishment is not severe; instead, it serves as a means of rectifying an action or decision taken. This approach of acknowledging our mistakes and rewarding our achievements allows us to maintain equilibrium in our decision-making process. It is crucial that rewards and consequences are oriented towards positivity, as maintaining a sense of equilibrium plays a vital role in effectively managing time.

Positive Skills

Positive skills can steer us towards a favorable outcome. Effective time management is achieved when we attain equilibrium and engage in productive learning activities, thereby utilizing our time wisely. Motivation is an additional valuable asset to possess on the path to success. Motivation is attained through various means, and certain elements in life possess the ability to influence our emotions and cognitive processes. Several factors that influence our levels of motivation include smoking, consumption of caffeine, insufficient physical activity, overindulgence in eating, poor dietary habits, and a limited capacity to adapt to changes. In order to foster motivation, it is imperative to prioritize the well-being of our minds and bodies, while strategically charting a path towards fulfilling our life's purpose. Acquiring proficiency in time management is imperative for all our endeavors in life. Since your earliest days, upon entering this world until your enrollment in school, you have actively acquired time management skills through various avenues, primarily focusing on self-development, which is essential should you aspire to establish meaningful objectives for your future. Failing to grasp our own individual identity will impede our ability to effectively manage our time. Please make efficient use of your time by embarking on the journey of learning.

The Detriments Of Time Management

Not formulating a strategic plan in a home-based business is tantamount to not formulating a strategic plan in any other type of business. A well-defined business model must be developed, a comprehensive marketing strategy must be implemented, and a strategic plan of action must be devised to achieve the objectives of the business. All of these factors are interconnected with the ability to effectively manage time, resources, and discerning effective strategies for the organization.

Engaging in daily planning may initially appear to require a considerable amount of effort, yet with consistent practice, it will eventually become second nature. Research indicates that on average, it requires twenty-one repetitions for an action to become ingrained as a habit. Once something becomes habitual, it becomes significantly easier to manage compared to when it is novel or in its initial stages.

Individuals engaged in home-based entrepreneurship enjoy utmost adaptability and convenience in carrying out their professional activities. There is no authoritative figure dictating their schedule, mandating tasks, prescribing deadlines, and dictating methods of execution, and so forth. Given the considerable liberty at hand, an individual lacking discipline will struggle to grasp the art of efficient time management or discerning when to refuse certain projects or new ventures.

For many entrepreneurs, they defer their work responsibilities or obligations for a variety of reasons. Engaging in this action has the potential to generate daunting levels of tension for the entrepreneur, precipitating a shift into crisis management mode.

Engaging in such work may give rise to further complications that could prove difficult to untangle or effectively handle. There have been instances of errors, unfinished projects, unachieved objectives, subpar work quality, and even subpar business outcomes.

Procrastination

What are a few of the primary factors that contribute to the procrastination tendencies of home-based entrepreneurs?

Why is it that they frequently defer their decision-making processes, embark on new initiatives at a later time, engage in expanding their business endeavors, or possibly delay the completion of significant projects that have the potential to generate further business opportunities for them?

Allow us to examine a few reasons as to why:

Dilly-Dally

The internet entrepreneur's work habits are of subpar quality.

The productivity of individuals engaged in home entrepreneurship with subpar work habits is typically sluggish, encompassing a delay in commencing tasks. They exhibit a tendency to consistently delay tasks and require extensive durations to complete projects or achieve objectives.

What potential outcomes could arise from the implementation of this online business endeavor?

Setbacks and downturns in the realm of commerce and revenue. In the event that they fail to meet a deadline or neglect to communicate with their customers or clients, it will lead to a negative impact on their business and a detrimental perception of their online reputation. This would be disadvantageous for individuals aspiring to become internet and web entrepreneurs.

On a regular basis, they also exhibit a tendency to procrastinate in various aspects of their lives, including personal matters, and are constantly striving to make up for lost time. This leads to the escalation of tension levels and a reduction in productivity levels.

The internet entrepreneur with subpar work habits is also under the belief that they perform better when facing challenges. Not truthful.

It is their belief that they will perform optimally when compelled to think rapidly, thereby stimulating their creativity. Not truthful. All of these factors ultimately contribute to their falling further behind with their tasks and exacerbating the existing tension. Period.

They consistently experience a sense of being overwhelmed. The internet entrepreneur who faces difficulties in the realm of efficient time management often appears to have made little progress. Many individuals frequently fail to take any action, regardless of whether they are proactive in their work or in completing tasks.

The overpowering feeling can also cause anxiety and therefore the propensity to form huge, expensive errors in their work. It is widely acknowledged that fatigue or overwhelming circumstances greatly increase the likelihood and magnitude of errors. Undoubtedly, this intensifies the perception of being overwhelmed and experiencing a sense of inadequacy.

Similarly, there is a prevailing sense of ineffectiveness observed in entrepreneurial ventures wherein individuals engage in procrastination. They express their wish for the task to be more manageable, given its immense scale, to the extent that doing nothing becomes a feasible option. In accordance with cyclical patterns, this phenomenon is expected to generate a spiral impact within the organization. Due to the failure of one task, a subsequent critical objective remains unfulfilled, thereby perpetuating the cycle and potentially exacerbating consequential challenges.

They perceive a necessity to attain perfection.

This particular trait stands out as one of the most pervasive and harmful attributes prevalent within a work-from-home business. To an exaggerated extent, they possess an unyielding belief in their need for perfection, employing all means necessary to avert any mistakes, ensuring precise outcomes from the outset, and striving relentlessly to fulfil the customer's every whim and desire with absolute precision. Not only is it impractical to hold such a belief, but it is also detrimental and unjust for the entrepreneur to have such expectations of himself.

Anticipating flawless execution could prove to be a misconception among digital business owners. It is highly unlikely that they will achieve perfection, and this unwarranted pressure they put on themselves exacerbates the situation.

Their desire encompasses the termination of projects, the fulfillment of deadlines, the accomplishment of objectives, all of which they aspire to achieve with unprecedented swiftness. However, the primary hindrance they commonly encounter is the initial inertia.

They may perceive their business endeavors as burdensome and dismiss them as inconsequential. This often engenders a sense of wellbeing as individuals become inclined to persuade themselves that if they themselves are not paramount, then they would be equally dispensable to their clients or purchasers. The entrepreneur will commonly postpone completion till the project meets their standards for perfection.

While the organization acknowledges this perception, it is often not acknowledged by their clientele. This inadvertently underscores the notion that it is an inefficient use of time, with unprofitable efforts expended toward a superfluous objective.

The entrepreneur exhibits an air of nonchalance or indifference.

Blasé? Is it a common occurrence for entrepreneurs in work reception to experience a sense of boredom? Indeed, they do! However, not in the conventional sense in which tedium is commonly employed.

They become indifferent due to a lack of innovation or variation in their work. While it is possible that they may find enjoyment in their current activities, they inevitably realize that performing the same tasks repeatedly becomes monotonous and devoid of any stimulating elements. Consequently, ennui ensues, resulting in a waning of interest in the tasks at hand.

Frequently, individuals who work remotely often express a preference for engaging in activities other than their job duties. Does this imply that they exhibit a lack of industry or diligence? Indeed, it is not uncommon for individuals to struggle with determining the appropriate starting point, organizational strategies, or effective approaches in initiating their business ventures and cultivating their professional aspirations. They may pursue alternative avenues for creative expression that do not pertain to business, such as participating in social media platforms or engaging in community forums, rather than dedicating themselves to their work diligently. Administrative obligations such as document handling or online tasks may supersede the actual execution of demanding work.

The entrepreneur will simply continue to delay the completion of tasks, longing for them to either inexplicably shrink in duration or vanish altogether. Their level of tension may escalate, as they become aware of the inevitability of this endeavor falling through, thereby rendering their tasks more perplexing to comprehend and objectives more challenging to achieve.

What outcomes have been produced by those snares? Is the individual adept at employing efficient time management techniques?

Making Lists

Organizing Your Life

An effective approach to time management involves the practice of creating and utilizing lists. There is empirical evidence to support the notion that creating lists can serve as an effective means of alleviating stress and anxiety. This is where the practice of anticipation and strategic task management becomes crucial.

Lists can greatly simplify tasks, as they eliminate any uncertainty surrounding the necessary steps and their respective order. The more efficiently you allocate your time, the greater capacity you'll have for accomplishing tasks.

By dedicating a brief portion of your schedule, whether it be prior to retiring for the night or upon waking in the morning, to compiling a list, you will ultimately accrue significant time-saving benefits. This not only proves beneficial for the completion of the required tasks, but also assists in addressing any additional duties associated with each respective task.

It is possible to create multiple lists. Such as:

Today's agenda encompasses a compilation of tasks that must be accomplished within the day.

Deferred task list - this constitutes a compilation of tasks that are of lesser significance but still need to be completed.

Additionally, it is possible to compile a comprehensive inventory of all the tasks that require completion.

For instance, consider a list of items typically found in a grocery store. In the absence of a specific checklist, what items comprise the contents of your shopping cart at the conclusion of your visit to the store? Most likely an assortment of items that were unnecessary from the outset. In the present circumstances, compiling a list would not only have served as a time-saving measure, but also as a cost-effective solution.

You have the option to categorize your list, which can enhance its manageability.

For Example:

Morning Noon Evening

Dispose of the waste Visit the post office Attend the gym session

Partake in the morning meal Acquire midday sustenance

Join Pam for dinner.

Alternatively, you may opt to record them chronologically, based on the priority of their completion within the daily schedule.

1. Take out trash

2. Have breakfast

3. Go to post office

4. Pick up lunch

5. Go to the gym

6. Have dinner with Pam

There exist numerous distinct approaches to composing lists. Simply ascertain which option is most suitable for your needs. Experiment with it until you are content with the outcome. Once you have compiled a list, the process of creating a schedule becomes notably more straightforward.

By consolidating the various lists, you will be able to formulate a comprehensive schedule. Prioritizing all of the listing activities will guarantee effective time management that aligns with your unique needs and requirements.

There is no universally effective approach, thus investing time in determining the most suitable method for oneself is the optimal course of action. Should your circumstances evolve, do not hesitate to modify an effective approach that you have discovered. The acquisition of adaptability is another valuable skill to possess.

The Significance Of Prioritization In Time Management

Efficient time management entails the timely completion of tasks, does it not? Accordingly, you have delineated your priorities, distinguishing between what is deemed significant and what is deemed less consequential. However, how frequently do you encounter circumstances wherein every single task on your agenda appears remarkably significant and requires immediate attention? What approach do you employ to distinguish between tasks of equal significance?

This chapter is devoted to assisting you in comprehending this fundamental principle of time management. Certain aspects, such as the formation of a comprehensive inventory, have been briefly addressed in preceding sections of the book. There is an abundance of intricate information to be found here.

Establish a Comprehensive Inventory

Prioritization occurs at varying hierarchical strata. Certain tasks must be completed today, regardless of circumstances. Subsequently, you harbor a specific set of objectives that are set aside for the duration of the week, in addition to a more extensive compilation that is to be completed prior to the conclusion of the month. In general, it is customary to reflect on one's accomplishments at the beginning of each day, week, or month, and affirm that all intended tasks have been successfully fulfilled.

Nevertheless, the actual correspondence between these lists falls short of the expected ideal. For example, you might think that a particular task is essential to be completed today itself. Nevertheless, attempting to assess its alignment with your weekly or monthly objective may be perceived as a daunting task. Thus, your daily priorities are usually derived from your overarching long-term objectives. Hence, it is essential that you commence with a comprehensive inventory.

Please record all of the tasks requiring completion. Ideally, your master list should consist of four columns comprising the serial number, task name, deadlines or due dates, and priority levels. The subsequent segments of this chapter will deliberate on several approaches to effectively prioritize one's tasks.

This shall serve as the primary repository for all of your work and activities. Once your master list has been prepared, proceed to divide the tasks into objectives that are to be achieved on a monthly, weekly, and daily basis. "In accordance with the matter at hand, the following course of action ought to be pursued:

Produce a monthly roster based on your comprehensive inventory.

The compilation of your weekly list is derived from the content of your monthly list.

Your daily tasks should align with the items mentioned in your weekly agenda.

Furthermore, it is important to refrain from becoming excessively preoccupied with itemizing every individual task while compiling these lists. Ensure that you prioritize the more significant task over the less significant one at every stage, working with deliberate intention.

Additionally, given the current circumstances, it may be prudent to evoke the 80/20 rule or the Pareto Principle. According to this principle, 20% of your efforts yield 80% of the outcomes. Instead of merely completing tasks on your checklist, strive to attain outcomes of this nature through your endeavors.

Please be advised that your master list will undergo continuous updates. It would be advisable to continue updating it. In pursuit of this objective, the utilization of a readily modifiable digital format will alleviate your workload.

Prioritizing Your Work

Failing to assign priority to your work will lead to a perpetual sense of being overwhelmed and continuously engaging in reactive problem-solving. Your master list functions as a dynamic and encompassing document that serves as a central repository, allowing you to both withdraw and deposit tasks based on specific circumstances. You are required to allocate priority to the activities mentioned in this list. This process of prioritization plays a pivotal role in effective time management.

While you are attending to your topmost tasks, please bear in mind the respective time frames or target dates associated with each assignment. Additionally, please bear in mind that certain tasks may require completion ahead of the designated deadline, particularly those that necessitate review and approval by a third party.

Furthermore, certain tasks may require input from individuals, necessitating the consideration of this aspect. Incorporating a follow-up with the relevant individuals may be necessary as an additional assignment, potentially. Presented here are several inquiries that require responses in order to accurately establish priorities:

Which tasks require immediate attention?

What are the potential consequences of failing to complete these tasks within the designated time frame?

What would be an suitable hour to commence working on the assignment?

What are the necessary inputs and resources that I require in order to successfully accomplish this task?

Which tasks remain incomplete that were expected to be finished by this point?

Please provide responses to the subsequent inquiries in order to establish a comprehensive record of your primary inventory, and subsequently modify your list of priorities.

What are the tasks or assignments that I have successfully undertaken?

What is the observable result of a task once it has been successfully executed? Does it align with expectations, or are there any modifications required?

Which tasks am I consistently delaying? What is the rationale behind my engagement in this activity?

Which items should not have been included on that list?

How might one curtail the master list?

Is this master list still relevant? Alternatively, should I place it in storage and create a fresh one?

Harness the Potency of the Eisenhower Matrix to Ascertain the Order of Importance for Your Tasks.

The Eisenhower Matrix was conceptualized by the ex-president of the United States, Dwight Eisenhower, with the purpose of facilitating the distinction between tasks of immediate significance and those of long-term importance. Essentially, imperative tasks necessitate your prompt attention. These forms of communication encompass electronic mail, telephonic conversations, text-based exchanges, and similar modalities. Significant responsibilities are those that contribute to the achievement of your long-term objectives. This matrix comprises a basic four-quadrant structure, featuring the following elements:

Crucial and significant - These tasks must be accorded the highest priority.

Tasks of significance but lacking immediacy - Allocate these activities in your calendar subsequent to determining your preferred timing for their completion.

Of minimal importance or urgency - Promptly remove them from your master list at your earliest convenience.

Tasks of immediate priority but lacking in significance - Shall be assigned to others (comprehensive guidance on delegation can be found within the section dedicated to this crucial aspect of time management).

Determine the Authentic Order of Importance for Each Task Utilizing the Ivy Lee Technique

Frequently, notwithstanding our utmost endeavors, we encounter difficulties in determining the precise hierarchy of significance among our daily assignments. The Ivy Lee method facilitates a thorough exploration and determination of the authentic prioritization of each task. This particular approach was devised over a century ago by Ivy Lee, a esteemed consultant in the field of productivity. Here are some guidelines regarding the functioning of this methodology:

Prior to retiring for the evening, it is recommended that you engage in the practice of documenting a list comprising six essential tasks that require your attention and completion on the following day. It is crucial to adhere to a maximum limit of six, and refrain from exceeding this number.

Please arrange these six items in descending order of significance and priority, with the most crucial one listed first and the least significant one listed last.

Commence with your initial task the following day. Devote your undivided attention to the task at hand, and only upon its completion, should you proceed to the subsequent undertaking.

Proceed with the execution of your agenda in this manner. Conclude the day by transferring any incomplete tasks to the agenda for the following day.

Engage in this task on a daily basis.

By limiting your list to a maximum of six items, you establish a compelling constraint that guarantees the inclusion of the most critical tasks. This methodology facilitates the discernment of the authentic precedence of every undertaking. Additionally, maintaining a singular focus on each task prior to proceeding to the subsequent one aids in enhancing your concentration. As a result, you can efficiently accomplish the task at a quicker pace, all while upholding the standards of excellence.

Strategy 7: Engage the services of a professional time management expert.

Leaders tend to make erroneous judgments in the absence of accountability. Engaging a manager for yourself would be a prudent decision. Allow him to determine your schedule and submit daily reports to your manager.

The paramount skill of any accomplished individual rests in their ability to exercise self-restraint. Nevertheless, you will discover that exercising self-control poses a greater challenge than commanding a military force. I strongly recommend that you consider the employment of a skilled "Time Manager". It is quite effortless to proceed with tasks when all aspects have been meticulously prearranged.

Your supervisor will schedule work days for you.

He will provide you with information and guidance regarding the upcoming meetings. He will assume the responsibility of overseeing unforeseen disruptions. Extract this concept from the pages of this literary piece. Seek assistance from a professional. Please request him to provide updates to you on a monthly basis, three times within each month. It shall not incur substantial costs in terms of both money and time.

Strategy 8: Acquire the Skill of Minimalism

"Let's examine the contents of a task agenda:

1. Rise early in the morning and engage in physical fitness activities.

2. Devote quality time to my family

3. Please ensure all emails and critical messages are thoroughly examined.

4. Place four essential telephone calls.

5. Compose the newsletter

6. Please proceed to the office and focus on completing my office assignment.

7. Schedule a meeting with my manager to engage in a conversation regarding the forthcoming meeting.

8. Additionally, the enumeration continues.

Do you possess a comparable agenda of tasks?

Could you please enlighten me as to which task in this list is most efficient in terms of productivity? Your personal involvement is necessary for both step two and step six. All remaining tasks have the potential to be delegated to external sources. Based on my estimation, it is likely that outsourcing could result in time savings of approximately 1-2 hours. You have the opportunity to participate in more significant undertakings during this period. This practice is commonly referred to as the art of minimalism.

There exists a distinction between machines and humans. Machines lack concentration. They are characterized by a deficiency in cognitive and affective capacities.

The human capacity for concentration is formidable. Focused attention is the path to attaining success in our particular circumstances. Under no circumstances should one divert attention to multiple objects concurrently. Engaging in multitasking leads to a 75 percent decrease in performance. By centering your attention on four objectives, your productivity undergoes a reduction of 16-fold.

Direct your attention to the crucial 20 percent and derive satisfaction from the consequential 80 percent outcomes.

It is a scientific concept supported by verifiable outcomes.

Strategy 9: Allocate Time for Unforeseen Interruptions

Setbacks and disruptions are inherent aspects of the human experience. Life would lack excitement in the absence of obstacles and challenges. One cannot evade challenges, and the identical holds true for disruptions encountered in the realm of professional pursuits. Existence is favorable as it encompasses both elation and adversity.

When considering the organization of your timetable, it is imperative to allocate time for unforeseen disruptions. Frequently, our intended plans fail to materialize. Your plan should possess sufficient adaptability to accommodate both time-sensitive milestones and unforeseen demands.

I have extensively experimented with various approaches to effectively cope with these unforeseen interruptions. Nevertheless, I have discovered just one approach that proves effective in the majority of instances.

Establish a specified duration for every instance of disruption.

As an illustration, suppose that your colleague approaches you with the intention of discussing pertinent matters.

Commence the discourse in the following manner,

Regrettably, this matter appears to be of significance, though I am only able to allocate a brief five minutes. Could we please defer this conversation to a later time? If that is not the case, kindly provide me with the essential aspects in a concise manner. Thanks."

An analogous declaration would suffice.

Time-Saving Strategy #2: Cease the Habit of Television Viewing

Cease your activity of occupying the space in front of the television and leisurely examining papers in advance of your professional obligations.

I have two underlying objectives for this matter: the first being that television and newspapers will criticize or depreciate your reputation. It will induce a negative emotional response, and in the case that individuals are discussing a recession, bank closure, or an incident of violence, it will initiate a pessimistic state of mind at the start of your day. Achieve something other than examining newspapers.

Television is a more unfavorable medium in comparison to print media since it consumes valuable time by airing programs, commercials, and news discussions.

If you possess a copy of the publication, I would encourage you to peruse the captivating sections comprising of puzzles, riddles, and Sudoku. However, I must admit that when it comes to the news content, I have little inclination to peruse the newspapers.

You may conduct an online search to access current news and swiftly acquaint yourself with noteworthy updates, provided any pertinent information catches your attention within approximately half a minute.

Kindly attempt this in order to verify the global shutdown within a span of approximately 14 days, as it is not unequivocally communicated to you at all times. Your life will essentially remain unchanged as it was previously.

Cable TV

I believe that it is not a mere coincidence that five years ago, I made the decision to discontinue my subscription to and utilization of digital television services. That marked the moment when my productivity increased significantly.

With the television, it is excessively effortless to sit down, change channels, and before long, a brief period of time has elapsed. If, by some remote possibility, all individuals were bestowed with immortality, the advent of cable television would undoubtedly represent a significant innovation. One should refrain from expending energy on watching television, as time cannot be reclaimed, be it tomorrow, last week, last month, or even last year.

I endorse the idea of engaging in viewing a DVD or partaking in a cinematic experience. The tendency to wander off and become easily distracted, particularly by advertisements, is certainly undesirable in my opinion. Cease the use of satellite television in your daily routine.

Efficiency Strategy #3: Implement Automated Systems for Coffee & Breakfast

Streamline the process of preparing your espresso and breakfast by automating them the evening before. Provided that you possess an espresso maker equipped with a timer function and subsequently take into account this circumstance, there is no necessity to prepare coffee in the morning. Arrange it for the preceding evening, and awaken to the soothing aroma of coffee.

Upon awakening, there is no requisite to place reliance on the machine's ability to gradually pour liquid into the container. Rather, one can pour a portion of liquid from a cup into their own cup or portable container.

Similarly, when it comes to breakfast, incorporating additional options or utilizing microwaveable breakfast items, such as pancakes, toasted waffles, or toast, can yield a time-saving of at least 1 minute per day.

Implement automation for the preparation of espresso and breakfast items the night before. The act of entering without depositing in the conduit, overloading, activating the button, incorporating water, or undertaking any necessary procedures, abstaining from such actions is, indeed, a time-saving measure.

One might consider, "I am gaining opportunity in the morning, however, I am losing time at night." As you complete tasks during the early hours of the day, and if you are in a rush, you would prefer not being concerned about dressing up, making toast, and activating the coffee machine. It would be advantageous if the majority of tasks adhere to scheduled timelines. This ensures that you are not burdened with multiple tasks and are able to maintain your focus. Strive to complete as many tasks on schedule, in advance, as feasible.

Incidentally, the acquisition of a Keurig coffee maker has proven to be one of the most favorable morning investments I have made in recent years. The price range on Amazon for different models varies from $67 to $167. One can acquire 'K-cup' cartridges, typically priced between 50 cents to 1 dollar per cartridge, and conveniently utilize them to prepare a cup of coffee or tea within approximately 3 minutes.

If you prefer chilled espresso or chilled tea, you have the option to fill a cup with ice cubes and mix directly on top of it. Alternatively, you can leverage the hot water feature to rapidly obtain boiling water for steeping tea bags or combining with instant oatmeal.

Time Wasting Habits

If the sole reason for our lack of productivity and time wastage was solely attributed to multitasking, it would not be as arduous to address the issue. Indeed, there exist a plethora of time-consuming behaviors that we might engage in, albeit unknowingly.

I have compiled a comprehensive inventory of eight prevalent behavioral patterns that individuals commonly engage in, wasting considerable amounts of time. Observe the numerous habits that you possess.

#1 - Allowing Distractions

In this era characterized by the vast inflow of information, it becomes an arduous task to quantify the sheer multitude of distractions permeating our surroundings. Indeed, distractions abound in every direction.

During our computer work, it is possible for pop-up advertisements featuring visually striking images to appear, thereby prompting us to click on them.

While addressing a client's email, it is possible that additional emails may be received, prompting us to commence perusing these newfound messages.

While occupying our workstation, an incident may arise where a literary publication adorns the surface of the desk, capturing our interest and prompting us to momentarily peruse its contents.

These are merely a handful of standard illustrations; however, the number of distractions is considerably greater, exceeding what can be comprehensively enumerated in this context.

#2 - Poor Planning

A well-structured plan serves as a guiding tool to enhance productivity and facilitate organization. One common error is when individuals attempt to allocate their time completely by scheduling appointments consecutively. They have scheduled a meeting from 10:00am-11:00am, followed by another meeting from 11:05am-12:00pm. They only give themselves 5 minutes between meetings, and if there are any delays, the whole schedule is thrown off.

#3 - Perfectionism

Perfectionism possesses a dual nature akin to the qualities of a double-edged sword. From one perspective, exhibiting an unwavering commitment to achieving perfection is highly commendable. Nevertheless, on occasion, the inclination toward perfectionism can result in an excessive expenditure of time in the pursuit of flawlessness within your tasks or endeavors, because:

Perfection is an elusive ideal that can never be fully achieved.

You allocate an excessive amount of time to complete the task.

You get stressed.

#4 - Delaying the completion of challenging tasks

It is quite common to postpone tasks when we perceive them to be arduous in nature. Frequently, we tend to prioritize simpler tasks, postponing the completion of more challenging ones. Taking a psychological standpoint, when confronted with two options that both entail pain, individuals tend to gravitate towards the option that presents a lesser degree of discomfort. This principle applies similarly when individuals are engaged in a compilation of duties.

Generally, the tasks that yield the most outcomes tend to require greater exertion to accomplish. I have been made aware of individuals expressing the following sentiment: "My inclination to prioritize simpler tasks is rooted in the fact that their completion provides me with a sense of fulfillment, affording me the perception that I am exerting productivity."

That assertion holds partial validity when one observes the completed tasks marked as accomplished in their task inventory. Nevertheless, it is imperative that the primary responsibilities are duly fulfilled, as the prolonged existence of these tasks on your agenda would only intensify the sense of pressure you experience.

#5 - Attempting to undertake all tasks independently

This behavior is closely associated with a lack of trust in others. If one possesses such a proclivity, it is likely that one holds the belief that others are incapable of performing the tasks with the same level of proficiency as oneself. It appears that you have a preference for allocating greater amounts of time towards personally handling tasks, as opposed to entrusting them to others. In order to enhance productivity, it is imperative to comprehend two fundamental aspects:

Each individual possesses proficiency in specific areas. Assign tasks in which you may lack proficiency to individuals who possess the necessary skills. Perhaps you possess strong planning skills but struggle with implementation and adherence? up. Therefore, it is advisable to assign the task of follow-up to individuals.

You are limited to a mere 24-hour day, and it is advisable to allocate your time towards tasks of utmost importance. Perhaps you possess adeptness in numerous endeavors; nonetheless, your temporal resources remain constrained. By engaging in a solitary pursuit of tasks, one is not effectively allocating time towards activities that yield the highest outcomes.

#6 - Avoid declining requests from family, friends, and colleagues

Do you experience difficulties in declining requests from individuals such as family members, acquaintances, and colleagues? It is likely that you aspire to exemplify kindness and avoid rejecting individuals. However, by consistently devoting your precious time towards assisting others, you may find that your availability for crucial responsibilities becomes limited.

It is imperative that you develop a certain level of resilience; assertively decline requests from others and effectively communicate your personal boundaries. This task may present initial challenges, but with practice, it will gradually become more manageable. Furthermore, as time progresses, your need to decline requests will diminish since individuals will increasingly discern your availability and willingness to assist.

#7 - Reviewing electronic correspondence and responding to telephone inquiries

How frequently do you ascertain your emails on a daily basis? In the past, I would frequently monitor my email inbox at intervals of approximately five to ten minutes. Now, I limit my email account usage to only one or two instances per day. Given that regular monitoring of emails not only consumes valuable time but also introduces disruptive elements.

By implementing time constraints on the handling of email inquiries, I am able to allocate a significant amount of additional time to concentrate on alternative tasks.

The identical situation applies to telephone conversations. If the call does not pertain to an urgent matter, I typically inform the caller that I will be contacting them at a designated time, allowing me to proceed with my ongoing tasks. Typically, I endeavor to respond collectively to any text messages received by employing the computer at a designated time. I establish a connection between my mobile device and computer, subsequently inputting and dispatching the messages through the computer interface. It is significantly more efficient in comparison to composing a message on my mobile device.

#8 - Has developed a dependency on online social networking platforms.

Facebook and Twitter serve as excellent platforms for establishing connections and facilitating information dissemination. They can also serve as significant detractors of time if one lacks the requisite self-discipline in their utilization. Establish a designated schedule for monitoring your social networking accounts and restrict your checking activities solely to that allocated time.

Upon initially commencing my utilization of Facebook, I experienced a profound sense of enthusiasm upon rediscovering individuals with whom I had previously lost contact. In seeking information about their well-being. I ultimately devoted the entire day to examining these websites.

If any of the aforementioned time-consuming habits are relevant to you, it is clear where your focus should lie. In order to eliminate an entrenched habit, it is necessary to cultivate a novel habit. In order to alter your tendency to waste time, it is advisable to cultivate behaviors that are both efficient and time-saving. Subsequently, I shall expound upon six discernible habits which have the potential to enhance productivity and yield time-saving benefits in the ensuing chapter.

Create Blocks of Time

For optimal achievement, it is necessary to have uninterrupted segments of time. The significance of your work directly correlates to the necessity of allocating specific time blocks for undertaking substantial projects.

You require a minimum duration of sixty to ninety minutes to successfully achieve any meaningful task. Approximately half an hour is required to fully engage one's cognitive faculties in undertaking intricate responsibilities, such as formulating a proposal, composing a report, or devising a crucial project plan.

After immersing yourself in the task, you may then devote your undivided attention, at an elevated state of consciousness and ingenuity, for the subsequent sixty minutes or more of concentrated and diligent work.

Do not blend artistic and managerial elements.

Combining creative tasks with functional or administrative tasks is not permissible.

One cannot effectively perform operational tasks and creative tasks simultaneously. They necessitate either swift or deliberate cognition, but not a combination of both. Efficient decision-making is imperative in the context of office activities, necessitating quick, short-range strategic thinking. Innovative endeavors necessitate cognitive processes, strategic preparation, and practical implementation.

Consider conceptualizing creative time as your "inner optimal period" and operational time as your "outer optimal period."

And refrain from conflating them. It is not possible to undertake substantial, innovative tasks that necessitate undivided attention and concentration within a conventional office setting without displaying a signage that states "DO NOT DISTURB" on the door.

How to Generate Segments of Time

Herein, I present a range of suggestions to establish concerted durations, each of which possesses the potential to markedly enhance your overall effectiveness and efficiency.

Initially, engage in work during the morning hours when you are in a state of heightened alertness and optimal cognitive functioning. Many highly productive individuals in the business field commit themselves to retiring early and then waking up at the hour of 5:00 or 6:00 A.M. This enables them to engage in uninterrupted work prior to commencing their daily duties at the office.

You will achieve a productivity level comparable to the average individual working in a conventional office setting within a span of three hours.

Another occasion that you can leverage to your benefit is the midday mealtime. This presents an excellent occasion for you to power down your mobile device, disconnect from the Internet, and eliminate any other sources of disturbance, while everyone else is absent from the office partaking in their midday meal. You will experience a serene and tranquil environment, wherein you can diligently focus on resolving some of your most crucial assignments.

Gain Extra Hours

An additional effective strategy that can be employed is to arrive at your office one hour prior to the arrival of other individuals. Utilize that hour to systematically structure your day and commence your tasks in advance of any potential disruptions. Subsequently, engage in work during the lunch period and achieve an additional hour of productivity. In conclusion, remain in the office an additional hour after everyone else has departed, utilizing this time to conclude your day and finalize your most crucial duties.

By modifying your daily routine in such manner, you effectively elude the traffic congestion during your commute to the workplace, as well as during your return journey. Consequently, three additional hours of productivity are incorporated into each working day. You achieve two, three, or even five times the amount of the average individual who adheres to a standard work schedule. By implementing this approach, you can increase your output twofold.

www.ingramcontent.com/pod-product-compliance
Lightning Source LLC
Chambersburg PA
CBHW050415120526
44590CB00015B/1973